A Call to Follow the Light

A Call to Follow the Light

Poetry Collection

1997-2016

Janice Kay Gainer

photography by Lori Younker

Published by CreateSpace in the United States of America. November 2016

ISBN 978-1-53908-576-8

Dedicated to
my beloved husband, Al,
our children, and grandchildren

TABLE OF CONTENTS

INTRODUCTION

 It was a cold December morning and I went downstairs for a cup of coffee and some quiet time. It was my 50th birthday, and I was feeling weary. I had been going through a difficult season in my life. I wondered why I was not feeling strong as I felt that I should. After all, I had been a Christian for many years and I thought that I should be handling life better.

As I sat there holding that cup of coffee, my mind wandered back to another morning. My husband and I were in Switzerland that morning, and had gone out for a walk at the base of the Alps. The terrain looked fairly flat compared to the towering mountains around us, but as we walked we realized it was a much steeper slope than we anticipated.

Later that day we boarded a cable car for a ride up to the very top of a mountain. How different it was to ride and enjoy the view than to climb a steep slope on my own. As I was thinking about this I felt the Lord speak to my spirit and tell me that I was making my life a steep climb by relying on my own strength and not really turning to Him. That morning I wrote the poem called "The Climb" because I wanted to remember what I learned that day.

That was the beginning of what now is this book of poetry. I have recorded in verse my personal discoveries in my quest to follow the light. These poems reflect the deeper understanding of my faith that I have found. They are for me a spiritual journal. Over the years I have shared these poems with other believers, and they have told me that they have helped them on their own journey to follow the Lord. It is my hope and prayer that they will encourage and in some way help you on your own journey.

In Christ's love,

Jan

The Climb

The traveler stared at the mountain's peak
With weary muscles and knees turned weak.
She had journeyed for so many years,
And now looking up her eyes filled with tears.

My youth is gone. My tired muscles ache.
Why do I have such a long climb to make?
Her companion watched her with a smile.
They'd been here before (though not for a while).

He watched her silently lift her pack
And set her feet on the rugged track.
He reached for the burden and offered his hand,
But she didn't notice as she busily planned.

It will be a hard climb today, she thought.
He mentioned again the ticket he'd bought,
And remembered times she'd been willing to ride,
And others when he'd walked like this by her side.

He tried again with a gentle word,
But his quiet pleas often went unheard.
So off they went to climb the hill.
It was useless to fight against her will.

He had to wait as he always would
For her to turn to him as she should.
She climbed and stumbled and fell and cried,
But never once turned to ask her guide.

As the day wore on she began to tire.
When she stopped to rest, he built a fire.
"Why are you climbing today?" was his query.
"You know it only makes you grow weary."

She looked at him and was filled with shame.
She had only herself for this hard day to blame.
He held out the ticket and picked up her pack.
She thanked him for gently bringing her back.

"Why do I do this?" she asked him once more.
"You forget that I'm here," he said, opening the door.
"The choice is yours to climb or to ride,
But either way I'll stay by your side."

"Why do you patiently put up with me?
I'm stubborn and willful and so slow to see.
One such as I can't bring you pleasure."
Jesus replied, " You are my treasure."

A Call to Start the Journey

I am a morning person. I always have been, even in childhood. Mornings are my favorite time. I like to get up early and often enjoy the beauty of the sunrise as the dark sky gradually grows brighter and brighter. So this is the time I choose for my quiet time. I make a quick cup of coffee and settle down with my Bible to just spend time with Jesus.

There are times when the awareness of His presence is so amazing, times when I feel bathed in love and acceptance. Not every quiet time is like that, but oh, how I long for those times. So I seek Him. I worship and wait before Him. I pour out my hurts, confess my failings, pray for others who need His touch, and I think. I think about the privilege that prayer is. Jesus bought access for us through His sacrifice on the cross. We can come before the Father with each prayer and our Savior is right there interceding for us.

At one time only priests could enter the tabernacle to come near the Lord. They alone brought the fragrant incense. Now our prayers bring that sweet fragrance to God, for that is what they are to Him, fragrance like the incense. When I think about the privilege that is given to me as a child of God, my heart overflows with thanksgiving and praise.

I felt that way early one morning and wrote the poem called "The Fragrance of Prayer." I hope you are exercising your privilege to pray, and I hope that you never cease to regard it as that, a privilege.

May my prayer be set before you like incense;
may the lifting up of my hands be like the evening sacrifice.
Psalm 141:2 NIV

The Fragrance of Prayer

In the soft, still quiet of morning, as the stars still light the skies
I wait with eager expectation as the sun begins to rise
Within my soul a longing exists that I cannot satisfy
No matter what foolish method I, in self-centeredness, might try

For this longing has been planted there and for many years has grown
Watered by tears of trials and fed by His precious Word alone
This longing is for sweet communion, for that fellowship above
For knowledge that my own prayerful praises
have pierced His heart with love

Oh, to worship Him fully with a heart so filled with grateful praise
Isn't that how we want to begin each of the rest of our days?
In the awareness of His presence, in the wonder of His love
Sending the fragrance of prayer to the true tabernacle above

Holy Spirit, stir my spirit, within me ignite the fire of praise
Let the pure passion of worship within my soul blaze
Help me offer acceptable worship in the name of my Lord and King
So all of my prayers and praises to His Father, He will bring

Forgive me all my trespasses, dear Lord, and let me join in the throng
That always sings before You. Let me sing the everlasting song
Receive this simple gift of worship that I desire to bring
Now with thanksgiving I offer it in gratitude to my King

Seekers of Light

Help us walk in the light of your presence
Lord, guide us to seek light all day long
For glorious light is your essence
Revealing weakness to make us strong

You're the Father of Lights and we praise you
And from you every good thing's bestowed
May the fire of your light always blaze through
All our lives as we travel this road

Change our lives to reflect the glory
That you've poured in our hearts from above
Give us boldness as we tell the story
Leading men to the light of your love

'Til frail bodies of dust are returned to
The earth when our days are all done
And with new eyes at last we behold you
In a world without moon, without sun

Where we'll dwell in the land of the living
When death's darkness has all passed away
And your glorious presence is giving
The true light we sought all of our days

Joyful Journey

Oh, come along with me, my precious friend
And we'll take a trip that will never end
We'll leave behind all we have ever owned
To follow the One who for our sins atoned

And on this joyful journey with our King
We have nothing to offer or to bring
He will provide for each invited guest
By His provision we'll be fed and dressed

High on mountain peaks or in valleys low
He'll walk beside us everywhere we go
In the desert, He'll teach us how to raise
The sweet sacrifice of our grateful praise

So come with me on this narrow way
Our journey begins again each new day
And in taking this trip we make the choice
That allows us in all things to rejoice

Lord of My Life

Oh, Abba, I love You, for You rescued me,
When my eyes were blind and I couldn't see,
Independent of You, doing all on my own,
Ruling my own life, seated on my heart's throne.

Oh, Abba, You called me, I knew You were there.
I didn't repent and follow You anywhere.
I knew of salvation, the gift of your grace.
I gave you my sins for You just to erase.

And I went to church and I worked and I tried,
But it was on me that I really relied,
Although from my sins I wanted acquittal
The real change in my life was very little.

Outwardly I knew how to play the church game,
Inwardly You knew I was really the same,
Conversations with You were infrequent and brief,
Trusting in You wasn't where I found relief.

My trust was in me in so many ways,
And from my unbridled tongue, You heard little praise
I can't comprehend why You can forgive me,
It took me so long to fall down on my knees.

But I'll ever praise You for You are my King,
Of Your grace and mercy I always will sing,
From the prison of self You're setting me free,
And Lord of my life is what You'll always be!

A New Beginning

Do you want a new beginning, a real fresh start
Do you want encouragement and hope in your heart
A chance to change and have a life that's new
Are you willing and wanting to find out what to do

What if this time you didn't try your solutions
And you made only one New Year's resolution
Resolve that you'll get to know Him who knows you best
What if this year this was your most heartfelt request

Lord, let me strive to know you better every day
Oh, let it be Yourself I seek for when I pray
And let me be willing to finally lay aside
The independent spirit that reveals my pride

Then make knowing and loving You the only goal
That is the deepest desire of my hungry soul
Let me seek You for Yourself, not for what You'll give
Completely change the way that I think and I live

Oh, what if you prayed that prayer each and every day
Do you think that your life would change in any way
Do you want a new beginning, a real fresh start
Then resolve that this year you'll give the Lord your heart

In Galilee or In Me

I wonder what it was like to sit on that hill
And listen to Jesus speak of His Father's will
There by the Sea of Galilee;
Or to push near to him begging, "Please!"
And feel His touch heal your disease,
Or sit as a child on His knee.

To have been on the Mount of Transfiguration
Must have been such an incredible sensation
As they beheld His glory;
Or to have watched Him raise Lazarus from the dead.
I wonder what all those who saw that did and said;
How they told their friends the story.

Yes, that was such a special time in which to live,
But I don't think I would really want to give
This day for one long ago.
Though like many I would have loved to see His face
To have that sight I wouldn't want to trade my place
For there is something I know.

There were some who saw Jesus then who couldn't see,
So I'm glad this is the time God chose for me
Though Galilee I couldn't roam.
For now I've become His dwelling place.
I hear His voice though I don't see His face.
My heart is now His home.

No, seeing Christ Jesus when He walked on this earth,

Would never have given this poor sinner new birth

Jesus had to die for me.

And for the rest of my life I just want to grow

To study, to seek, to love, to follow and know

The One Who set me free.

The Price of Grace

Suffering and sorrow, indescribable loss
Both the Father and Son endured the cross
The expensive price of grace
Agony inflicted upon God's beloved Son
Agony for the Father who watched as it was done
As He let Him take our place

Jesus felt the sweat drops of blood flow from His brow
And prayed that the cup might pass away somehow
In Gethsemene's garden
And His Father listened to each painful word
Every sweat drop was seen; every plea was heard
And yet He bought our pardon

And the Son chose to accept His Father's will
To suffer and to die and to let His blood spill
He endured such scorn and shame
We've been made holy and blameless in His sight
Moved from our darkness into His marvelous light
What a privilege we claim

Suffering and sorrow, indescribable loss
May we never take lightly the cost of the cross
Sin should bring tears to each eye
For though our glorious Lord will always forgive
It's a life of holiness we should strive to live
For each sin caused Christ to die

A Call to Faith

One Christmas I received a delightful gift from a friend, a music box shaped like a treasure chest. When the music box is opened to play, a nativity scene comes up from inside the box. What a perfect picture this makes of the true treasure all of us find in our precious Savior, Jesus Christ. Looking at this little music box one day made me think about all of the other things we spend our lives pursuing, things that in the end we discover are really not as important as we may have once believed.

It is easy for us to get caught up in the race to gain more money, power, or praise. After all these are the things greatly valued by much of our society. We are led to believe that happiness will be ours if we are wealthy or famous or powerful. But, all we need to do is look at the lives of many celebrities who have attained these and yet have not found that happiness and fulfillment.

Those of us who have found our way to Christ and have placed our faith in Him do find peace, and joy, as well as fulfillment. Life takes on deeper meaning, and we know what really matters is learning to love our Creator, trusting Him as we journey through life, and seeking His glory in what we do. We are slowly transformed into people of faith and prayer. We learn to think more about others and less about ourselves. Strangely, the more we seek to give to others and to honor God, the more happiness we find for ourselves.

The result of this time of reflection as I listened to the music box play is the poem I call "Treasure." I hope that you will enjoy it and that it will cause you to reflect on the true treasure available to you in Christ.

These have come so that your faith—of greater worth than gold, which perishes even though refined by fire—may be proved genuine and may result in praise, glory, and honor when Jesus Christ is revealed.

1 Peter 1:7 NIV

Treasure

Mankind is on a continuous treasure hunt
Fueled by gargantuan greed and unmet want.
We know there's a buried chest full of jewels and gold
And many are still on the search when they grow old.

Yes, our lives can become one long, unending quest
For that magical, mystical, illusive chest.
That chest full of power or men's praise or money
That chases the storm clouds and makes each day sunny.

But if we obtain power and praise and money,
The emptiness we feel is not very funny.
How could we be so blind? We would never have guessed
That we'd wasted our lives while pursuing the chest.

So, then, is there no treasure? Is it all a lie?
Are we born just to seek? Do we live just to die?
No, the treasure is real. There's an end to the quest.
There's even a map to guide us to the right chest.

But, when we read the map and all the directions,
We still can have questions and even objections.
This can't be the treasure, the goal of existence
And holding the map, we still put up resistance.

For the map is the Bible. God is the treasure

And only in Him is there joy beyond measure.

And the cost of this treasure's the life we each live.

He won't take it from us. We each must choose to give.

But when we give Him our lives, then at our request

He will pour out the contents of the real treasure chest.

And then into each soul will flow riches untold.

He's more precious than silver, more costly than gold.

The Way

I sought to find the way to God
I traveled countless roads
And upon my burdened shoulders
I added countless loads

I stacked them high and tied them tight
Secured with heavy rope
I staggered through the dark of night
Without the light of hope

The harder that I sought the way
The more my load increased
And I remained a prisoner
Who yearned to be released

But that was then and this is now
My heavy load is gone
The dark of night is left behind
I've walked into the dawn

Now I don't seek the way to God,
Some formula or plan
Instead I simply spend my time
As any seeker can

I talk to Him with faith He hears

Christ bought that right for me

And I believe His word is truth

And I believe I'm free

There is no route to get to God

Unless you kneel and pray

Independence always stops the trip

For Jesus is the Way

Not Everyone Who Says, Lord, Lord

Is it possible to be unaware
That though in a wheat field, you're a tare?
Do many who weekly fill church pews,
Of their soul's condition have no clues?

I wonder if there are demons who gloat
O'er some supposed sheep who is a goat?
Lord, Lord, it says they will one day cry.
Ever knowing them, He will deny.

It is faith that saves and not what we do,
But real faith causes real action, too.
Want to avoid the Judge's sentence?
Then be sure you've known real repentance.

Take a look at your own attitude.
Is it one of humble gratitude?
Are there God-made changes in your life?
Just ask your husband, ask your wife.

Do you have the courage, have the nerve
To ask yourself whom you really serve?
There will never be a sadder defeat,
Than that of tares who thought they were wheat!

Divine Embrace

Have you ever felt a divine embrace
Or been carried into the holy place,
Where you met with the Lover of your soul,
And let Him make you completely whole?

Or are you pondering infinity,
Trying to understand the Trinity?
Theologians and scholars struggle so.
I'll tell you a secret, just let it go!

Take a leap of faith into God's open arms.
He will catch His child. You won't come to harm.
And then you'll enter into peace and rest.
With forgiveness and love you will be blessed.

Just accept the purchase Christ has made.
You are free from debt. Your bill has been paid.
There's nothing left for you to do or say.
If you want to be free, there's just one way.

Call out to God and be carried away.
Don't wait for tomorrow. Go there today!
Leave it all behind. Quit life's hectic race.
Be enfolded in that divine embrace.

Reason to Sing

My hope is in you, the Ancient of Days
High King of Heaven who's worthy of praise
I call You all day long
Protect me now as I struggle and strain
Resisting the devil and fighting the pain
I sing You a new song

I picture You hearing each note I raise
Each faith-filled, trusting word of praise
Feeling the love I bring
Give me a true and undivided heart
So that in heaven's choir I may take part
And please You as I sing

For all of my being cries out for You
As millions of others are crying out, too
Great is Your love toward me
For in all of those voices You hear my own
And grant me complete access to Your throne
You always hear my plea

I recall Your great and marvelous deeds
And the way that You supply all my needs
I remember Your grace
For nothing compares to the God who lives
And continually loves and gives and gives
His light in this dark place

So no matter how dark and dismal it seems

I'll always have hope and always have dreams

You withhold no good thing

And from strength to strength I can move each day

If I will just reach out to You and pray

There is reason to sing

Remember His Love

Keep quiet, be still, just be patient and at rest
Keep counting as joy this inevitable test
It caught you off guard this unexpected blow
But stand firm now and just let your faith show

Remember the times you've been amazed by His grace,
Times when God has helped you face what you couldn't face
Days He carried you through things when you felt so weak
Times when in your heart, you knew you heard Him speak

Remember His love and all His promises, too
If you do, I know that you will make it through
And you will be stronger than you were in the past
It's not your first trial, and it won't be your last

But one thing is certain; you know that you will stand
For you are safely upheld by His strong, right hand
You are His precious child; He'll never let you go
And you know that's the truth for He has told you so

A Call to Growth

I wrote "Robes of Righteousness" because of the struggle that I went through in learning to believe that I have been given the righteousness of the Lord Jesus Christ in exchange for my own filthiness. One of the greatest impediments to my understanding of this great exchange had to do with a particular sin of which I am guilty. I am a divorced woman. Although I have been blessed with a wonderful marriage to my second husband, Al, for almost 40 years, it is nonetheless a fact that I have been the wife of two men.

It is true that God hates divorce, and I understand far too well the devastation it causes in the lives of all involved. I watched my children and stepchildren suffer the consequences of living in a broken home.

Consequently, I had a hard time in my early years as a Christian believing that God could love and forgive me, a woman guilty of this failure.

When my first husband left, I literally thought my heart had been broken and that I would never feel whole again. I found my peace in the love of Christ, but in the body of Christ, it is sometimes difficult to be guilty of this particular sin. It doesn't matter what your interpretation is of the Scriptures surrounding the limitations to church leadership and ministry by those who have had more than one mate.

In the end, the struggle I went through was not the fault of varying theological positions on this issue. The problem rested in my own failure to trust that the payment of Jesus Christ at Calvary had washed away every sin in my life, including the sin of divorce. I took the arguments against remarriage and service in particular positions such as that of deacons to heart. Somehow I felt unclean. I didn't doubt that I would spend eternity with the Lord. However, I did doubt that He saw me as completely clean. I felt that this sin was forever a wall between me and the Lord that I love.

This was no small struggle in my life. I grieved for years, and it was the greatest obstacle I faced to freedom in Christ. I want to say that I don't blame anyone for my difficulty. The responsibility rests squarely on my shoulders. The Bible says many things about which Christians have debated for centuries, but it is very clear about the source of our righteousness. It comes from Christ alone.

If I am dressed in the righteousness of Christ, my robe will not be a dingy shade of gray. The sins I have committed are not an issue. I am not going to stand before God wearing anything but the pure, white, righteous robe of Christ. I would never have any hope on my own, so no matter what the correct interpretation about the life here on earth of divorced Christians may be, it is true that it has no impact whatsoever on God's love and acceptance of me. He hasn't singled those of us who are guilty of being divorced out and labeled us as unacceptable. He can't see that or any of the multitude of other sins I or other Christians have committed without seeing them filtered through the blood of the perfect Lamb. I am so grateful that He loves me in spite of myself and that someday I will wear the blazing white linen of my precious Lord.

Robes of Righteousness

In robes of righteousness arrayed
Completely pure and blameless made
By the sacrifice of God's begotten Son
Boldly, I may approach His throne
His righteousness claimed as my own
Of all my spots and blemishes, He sees none

Though some may say stains of my past
On my garments, dark shadows cast
My dear Father sees such filthiness no more
As the daughter of Heaven's King
To His holiness I will cling
And reject all the sin-stained rags that I wore

I'll agree, I deserve great loss
But He paid my debt on the cross
He pronounces charges against me withdrawn
Satan can't impose his own sentence
For I've been cleansed through repentance
All the stains of past sins are forever gone

In robes of righteousness arrayed
Incomparable grace is displayed
No matter what stains some may think they see
So I'll still choose the attitude
That shows God all my gratitude
And see myself just as clean as He sees me

Knowing God

There is an indescribable peace
That brings to the heart and soul release
From every painful thought
It's a peace the world cannot provide
Given to those who in Christ abide
A peace that can't be bought

It does not come with power and wealth
Or beauty or passion or robust health
Though men seek after these
It doesn't come through knowledge or skill
Or food or drink or some magic pill
Nor from people we please

This joyful peace in the midst of strife
Is there when Christ becomes your life
When you've proved His love for you
When the winds of change bluster and blow
But like a firmly planted tree you grow
Whatever you're going through

Trials will come and trials will go
Winds of change will continue to blow
That's just the way things are
But if you know the God you serve
You'll stand firm and not lose your nerve
You are equipped for war

So seek to prove and find Him true
He's wonderful, loving and good to you
He's never ending love
He's sovereign Lord of all there is
And all the power and might are His
But He's gentle as a dove

He'll never change; you can be sure
He alone is holy and completely pure
And you can trust His Word
Although He's just, He gives you grace
And He meets His children face to face
Your every prayer is heard

He knows everything there is to know
He's on mountains high and in valleys low
He's the omnipresent One
He's your source of power, joy and peace
The One who gives you sweet release
The God you need to know

For knowing Him must be the goal
Of every seeking, searching soul
It's what we're here to do
So think about all you've seen and heard
Draw near to Him and study His Word
He will draw near to you

Prison of Pride

"For me to live is Christ," wrote Paul.
I didn't understand that at all.
For me to live was struggle and strain,
Locked in my self-made prison of pain.

Though Christ had died my soul to save,
I didn't feel like I was his slave.
I'd heard the slaves of Christ were free,
But that didn't make any sense to me.

"We're bondslaves", stated both Paul and James.
I found it hard to apply their claims.
For I was sure that it had to be
Just saints like these who were slaves but free.

I thought on my inadequacy,
From God I had no expectancy.
"I can't live this life," I cried out loud,
"I know, my child, you're much too proud.

"Proud?" I said and was really shocked.
"Is that what has my prison locked?"
Yes, in your pride, you try to do
What only I am able to do.

You must admit all your need for Me

I'll make you my slave and set you free.

You've nothing to offer, nothing to give.

I am your life, now gratefully live.

Come Unto Me

Come unto Me, Christian. I am calling you.
Come and humbly follow. I'll show you what to do.
We'll spend some time alone. I'll speak and you will hear.
I am always with you. I always will be near.

I'll cleanse your heart and change you as you follow Me.
Come unto Me, Christian. Come and you will see.
I've placed My yoke upon you. It's easy and it's light.
At least for those who follow and don't put up a fight.

But if you push ahead, departing from My side
Full of independence and selfish, sinful pride.
You'll find life's a misery; by problems you'll be choked.
You cannot live apart from Me. We are firmly yoked.

And if you will not listen when I say, "Go there!"
You'll find life's a burden too difficult to bear.
Those who do not follow feel I'm dragging them along
And hearts are filled with sorrow that should be filled with song

But if you'll walk beside Me and let Me set the pace,
You'll walk or run with gladness and learn to live by grace.
Come my chosen child, become a child blessed.
Do not be so weary when I can give you rest.

Come unto Me, Christian, I've given you My name.

So come and follow Me and never be the same.

Be broken and be yielded, surrendered unto Me.

Realize the yoke that binds us is the yoke that sets you free.

A Different Sword

Ready to fight when evil attacks
To quickly return more evil back
Oh, it's so natural to do
So I cause you pain like you caused me
Oh, I'll show you just you wait and see
It's so sad and yet so true

But we must learn a different way
A lesson taught in the garden that day
To men so ready to fight
The Lord corrected their reaction
He wouldn't allow their distraction
And made them do what was right

The swords were then put back in their place
And Jesus went on to face
All that He had come to do
He quietly took their vicious abuse
And all the rage on Him turned loose
He did this for me and you

And so now our choice must be clear
It's not others that we have to fear
But evil in our own hearts
So carefully listen for God's voice
He's telling us to make that choice
Freedom comes when obedience starts

So, friends put your swords back in their place

Not evil for evil, just give grace

And then the world will see

People who live by a different sword

The sword of the Spirit, God's own Word

And his truth will set you free

A New Fire

Touch me, Lord with the Spirit's Fire
And flood my heart with deep desire
To yield my life to You.
Open my eyes that I may see
The Glorious One who beckons me
To live a life that's new.

In reverent awe may I stand
Laying aside all I have planned
And seek the course You chose.
In brokenness face all my sin,
Let a new way of life begin
As your Spirit in me flows.

Open my ears to hear your voice
That with all my being I rejoice
Just to know You are near.
Let others see a change in me
That helps them, too, to be set free
From anything they fear.

Use my lips, my hands, my feet
To bring your love to all I meet
With wisdom from above.
Change me, Lord, your will be done
Let victory over self be won
Through the power of your love

Abiding in His Love

Father, teach me to sow, sweet seeds in peace,
That the fruit of righteousness may increase.
May Your wondrous love in me be shown
By seeds that are in obedience sown.

May I have precious moments to treasure
When my hungry heart can feel Your pleasure;
Then bask in the light shining from Your face,
And feast fully on Your amazing grace.

Give me those times when my soul's cup You fill
With the joy that comes from doing Your will;
Those tender times when from deep down inside
My spirit knows that in Your love I abide.

Oh, Father, though I struggle to obey
Give me courage to choose Your will today.
Apart from You, Lord, nothing can be done
But with Your helping hand my battle's won.

Only You can cause my spirit to grow
But show me the seeds that I need to sow.
May the fruit of Your Spirit come to be
Produced as submission is taught to me.

Unaware

In the shadow of God's mighty wings
A weary warrior fearfully clings
To the promise of His word
The shadow is hidden from his sight
From his hiding place, he thinks it's night
Hot tears have his vision blurred

Though those mighty wings protect him there
He doesn't see and he's unaware
He thinks God is far away
So blinded by his self pity and fear
He believes things are as they appear
A dark, dismal shade of gray

But in truth there is no better place
Then beneath the shadow of God's grace
Though it takes some faith to see
So many a Christian shivers with dread
When he could be praising God instead
For he's right where he should be

But now and then; Yes, once in a while
He may look up and have to smile
At what that viewpoint brings
And at the sight his fears quickly fade
For he sees he's only in the shade
Of his Father's mighty wings

A Call to Worship

Worship is such a joy and such a privilege. I'm sure I didn't always feel that way, but now there is nothing sweeter than singing praises to the Lord. When I join with other believers in celebrating what is ours in Christ, gratitude overflows my heart. I love to lift my hands in praise. For me it is a sense of reaching up toward my Father as little children reach up to a loving parent. It is also a symbol of my surrender to his lordship in my life. I'm acknowledging that I trust Him completely.

Worship is a time when I am able to express the joy of my salvation and the deep love that I have for the One who died for me. There are moments of reverence in worship when I just want to kneel before Him. Other times there is such joy that I feel like I am dancing inside. I'm filled with delight as I sing to Him.

I know that I am limited in my understanding of our Creator, but my heart's desire is to know Him more and to live a life to His honor and glory. I will be on this journey to seek to know the one who knows and loves me best all of my life. I wrote the poem called "Upon the Wings of the Wind" one day when I just felt extremely close to the Lord in worship, a day when I sensed the presence of the Lover of my soul in a very close and tender way. When I read this poem, I remember that precious time with the Lord and so this poem is a personal favorite of mine.

> *He lays the beams of His upper chambers in the waters;*
> *He makes the clouds His chariot;*
> *He walks upon the wings of the wind.*
> Psalm 104:3 (NASB)

Upon the Wings of the Winds

Upon the wings of the winds is where He walks
The Lover of my Soul who in my heart talks
And tells me of His sweet love
Then my hands reach up to Him for I must raise
From this heart that is His my passionate praise
Offered to heaven above

Upon the wings of the winds my spirit sings
And gratefully runs and soars and laughs and clings
To the One I live to know
Though I can't know Him yet as I one day will
Still as I worship He lets me drink my fill
And sets my heart aglow

Upon the wings of the winds we'll one day meet
Then I'll gratefully cast my crown at His feet
And know Him as He is
But until that great day when the trumpet sounds
And all of my being His glory surrounds
My hands still reach up for His

The Heart of a Worshipper

The heart of a worshipper, oh that's what we desire
A heart that for the love of God flames with passion's fire
The kind of heart that reaches up for the Lord's embrace
And ever finds admittance into the holy place

We want a heart that dances with abandon at His throne
And sings in every circumstance because we are his own
The kind of heart that beats with compassion for the lost
And gives itself to God's call and doesn't count the cost

How do we get that heart? What exactly does it take?
Be aware to get such a heart requires yours to break
Then all the broken pieces must be placed in God's hand
To do with as He wishes and as He alone has planned

When there are no pieces that you've chosen to withhold
He'll mend your heart and fan the flame that never will grow cold
And you'll worship with a heart of love for all the world to see
The true heart of a worshipper--broken, healed and free

Refrigerator Pictures

Refrigerator pictures, childish works of art
Displayed in the kitchen, they touch a parent's heart
Cute, crayon creations hung there with pride and joy
Because of the love for a little girl or boy

With scribbles and smudges and figures not quite right
We always find their efforts precious in our sight
And when a child gives something made with tiny hands
The worth of such gifts every parent understands

Like refrigerator pictures are things we do
Words that we have written and songs we've sung to You
Childlike attempts, praises not quite right
Lord, we hope You find them precious in Your sight

Not unlike small children's tiny unskilled hands
Is our limitation to truly understand
But You are our Father, so our poor offerings
Can be considered worthy by the King of Kings

Like refrigerator pictures hung there with love
Are gifts of prayer and praise we send to You above
We know we can't offer a master's work of art
But we hope our efforts still touch our Father's heart

Victory

Oh, Author and Perfector of the faith I hold,
Worker of miracles and more precious than gold,
Full of compassion, full of mercy and of grace,
Bring your light in the darkness of this sin-filled place.

Creator of the universe, holy and just,
It's only in you that I am able to trust;
And only in You can I make sense of this life,
Or cope with my struggles and endure all the strife.

You're the Light of the World, my Provider and King,
The One who can cause me in my sorrow to sing,
The One who is my Guide as I journey this road
From You every good and perfect gift is bestowed.

My Healer, my Helper, my Defender, and Friend,
You'll never leave me. You'll be with me to the end.
My Savior, Redeemer, the Sacrificial Lamb,
You're worthy of all worship. You are the I Am.

You'll perfect, confirm, strengthen, and establish me,
And from the mouth of the lion, You will set me free,
If I resist Satan and I draw near to You,
I can have victory in what I say and do.

But that victory is Yours. I'd die on my own.

I'd fail every minute were Your power not shown;

For I am a vessel that is fragile and weak;

And so for this day it's Your help that I seek.

Hold me and then help me to take captive each thought,

And apply all the lessons that I have been taught.

Then let me be grateful as I recognize Who

Is living in victory's not I, Lord, but You.

Singing His Song

There are lyrics God writes

To be sung both day and night

And He calls me to come sing along

Not a song that I can hear

With the use of my own ear

For my heart sings the notes of this song

I'm still learning the right beat

As I kneel down at His feet

For I haven't practiced singing that long

And to my weak melody

He brings strong harmony

As I struggle to sing out His song

Though I am often off key

He's always patient with me

And corrects all the notes that are wrong

Though I have poor syncopation

He still gives an ovation

When my heart sings the notes of His song

There's a part still unsung, too

For it's written just for you

And he wants you to sing it out strong

So come join in the chorus

For our Father adores us

As our hearts sing the notes of His song

Name Above All Names

When I listen and I hear the sweet sound of his name
There is no sound on earth that can stir my soul the same
I love to hear it. I love the sound.
Love that pulses deep within the chambers of my heart
Where the senses of my soul know that from the start
That's the name that turned my world around

When I whisper it in worship, or sing it out in song
It's the bearer of that name that makes my spirit strong
I love to hear it. I love his name.
For when it falls from my lips or resounds in my ears
I remember how that name releases me from fears
He bore all my sin. He bore my shame.

When I'm taunted by the one who torments me with lies
It's the blessed name of my Lord, my tortured soul cries
I love to say it. It sets me free.
For fighting dark powers, I've no weapon of my own
But the Lover of my Soul won't let me fight alone
The Name above all Names fights for me

When I live for myself and go my own stubborn way
He forgives me and loves me when in his name I pray
Oh such sweet comfort, He lets me know.
So for all the future days that still lie out ahead
By the bearer of that name, may my steps all be led
His name is Jesus. I love it so.

Image of a King

When the image of Christ my mind longs to see
A picture of a carpenter comes to me,
A sweet, gentle soul in robe and sandaled feet,
Someone my poor heart doesn't tremble to meet.

But is this the Christ who is alive today?
It is not who John met on Patmos that day
Messiah of Israel, the Holy One,
The Risen Christ, Lord Jehovah's mighty Son.

I know why the carpenter is my mind's choice,
And not this King with rushing waters in his voice,
With eyes like fire and head and hair like snow,
A sharp sword in his mouth and bronze feet that glow.

And yet I think I really should try to see,
The powerful God who chose to die for me.
The one who holds the stars in his hand
Is the one who my own redemption has planned.

He who shines like the sun at its brightest time
Is the one who offers us heaven sublime.
If I look at who Jesus Christ really is,
I'll be more grateful to know that I am His!

Heart Song

Now behold your God, the sovereign King
Who is in control of everything
Know your God and then in peace be still
Nothing can happen outside His will

Mountains, depths, seas, and dry land
All came into being by His hand
He controls the lightning, wind, and rain
From your hands He has nothing to gain

All might and power are in His hand
And your great God no one can withstand
No bribe will He accept from you
He'll do just as He chooses to do

In whatever He does, you will be blessed
For His will for you is always best
So have no more fears for tomorrows
You'll have His peace within your sorrows

So count it all joy when trials start
Remember He's there, right in your heart
And when you're weak, He'll still be strong
From your broken heart will come His song

A Call to Follow the Light

The world has some strange ideas about beauty, and it is easy for us to be overly concerned about our appearance especially in a culture like ours that puts so much emphasis on the physical. For the Christian woman though, beauty is not about externals although all women like to feel attractive and to wear things that make them feel pretty. I think that's just part of our femininity. But beauty fades. Time takes its toll on our bodies, but there is beauty that grows with time and in spite of everything that life sends our way.

Over 40 years ago I met the Lord Jesus Christ in a little Southern Baptist Church, and on that very special day, I also met a woman who became my very close friend. We were young wives in our twenties, with our lives out in front of us and with no idea of the trials we would face over the next 3+ decades. We also had no concept of how little we knew about the Lord who saved us, and how much walking with him would change our lives.

I remember the silly things we said and did in our youth, and I remember our physical appearance. Skin that wasn't wrinkled, chins that hadn't multiplied and drooped, and legs that didn't look like a road map of blue veins. I particularly remember my friend Nancy's beautiful, thick, dark blonde hair. I used to cut her hair for her and was always amazed at how thick and easy to style it was.

I had no idea that 30 years later, I would sit in my backyard combing out thick clumps of that lovely hair as the ravages of chemotherapy took their toll. We sat there together, and there were both tears and laughter. Nancy kept her humor and her joy in Jesus through it all. She turned from the falling hair and suggested we take a drive to enjoy the beautiful spring day, and we did. As we did she pointed out the beauty of the flowering dogwood trees all around.

Nancy asked if I'd ever noticed how dogwood trees seem to have their branches all tilted up. She said she had heard that it was because the larger oaks and other trees around them tend to block so much of the light and that the little dogwood trees have found a way to get as much light as they can by pointing their branches up toward the sky. "Jan," she said, "I think that's how we have to be. We have to continually keep reaching up to the Lord to find his light no matter how dark our days seem." I looked at Nancy with bald spots all over her head and thought how beautiful she was. She was reflecting the beauty of her Lord and nothing could overshadow that.

When Nancy went to sleep that night, I stayed up and wrote the poem "Nancy's Song" about our experience that day. You see over a lifetime of knowing Christ, Nancy learned that what's really important isn't what we look like or what we have to wear, or even if we have our health. She learned that she had Jesus and no matter what happened to her, He would be there with her and he would make something beautiful out of it. Nancy fought and lost a difficult battle with cancer. Her hair grew back in and then fell out again when she had to face even stronger chemo as the cancer advanced. Pain came, and she faced a great deal of suffering.

And yet, just as she had throughout our 30+ year friendship, she shared her love of Christ with those who don't know Him, she taught his Word to younger women and to little children, she shared the musical gifts and talents God had given her, and it is my personal opinion that she had a beauty that no worldly adornment could ever come close to matching. I wish you all the beauty that a close walk with Jesus can bring to you. Grow in his beauty and one day you will be ready to meet Jesus as the Bride of Christ, dressed in His righteousness, and clothed in garments that are whiter than snow.

Nancy's Song

The hills in Missouri are covered in white
The annual springtime spectacular sight
That always brings joy to my heart
For Father you placed within all mankind
A response to creation to beauty we find
So in springtime we, too, can take part

The hills that display this spectacular sight
Do so because of tiny blossoms of white
On every flowering dogwood tree
Tiny trees overshadowed, kept covered in shade
Like the shadows of trials that my life pervade
That seem so overwhelming to me

The dogwood's not daunted by oaks that surround
And blooms right where she's planted in hard, rocky ground
For this tree's discovered how to find light
And as I look closely, her secret is clear
I smile and remember I've nothing to fear
I, too will wear a garment of white

Like the dogwood whose branches all point to the sky
I know how to find light and so that is why
My own hands are uplifted in praise
And I will keep reaching to you on my way
I know you will hear me each time that I pray
You'll surround me with light all my days

The River of His Delights

My thirsty soul cries to You, Father of Lights

May I drink from the river of Your delights

May my parched soul be quenched

Though I'm weary and tired, give me Your sweet rest

By Your mercy and grace I know I'll be blessed

In Your love's rain I'm drenched

Though I've tossed and turned through many troubled nights

I awake at the river of Your delights

In acceptance I immerse

And You wash away every doubt and fear

Take away all shame and make my conscience clear

Then I praise You in verse

For nothing on earth or in heaven above

Can wash sin-filled hearts but Your river of love

Or quench a thirsty soul

I pray for others who battle through dark nights

Let dawn deliver Your river of delights

Where broken hearts heal whole

They feast on the abundance of Your house;
You give them drink
from Your river of delights.
Psalm 36:8 NIV

Light the World

Lord, let me make a difference. Let me be light,
In a world blind from sin in their darkness and night.
Help me live what I say about all I believe.
I look at my life and it makes my heart grieve.

I've lived in this land that has denied You for years,
Yet I look at my neighbors and I don't shed a tear.
Though they walk in the dark while I say I have light,
I'm just concerned with myself and not with their plight.

I'm as busy as they with the folly of play.
I entertain myself when I should fast and pray.
In a church filled with hundreds, Your light flickers low.
Yet we're the light of the world. Your Word tells us so.

Lord, forgive me and others who are called by Your name;
And change us completely. We can't stay the same.
Lift us out of our sin; give compassionate hearts.
We can't change the past, but let us make a new start.

I know that we're weak, but I know You are strong.
It's You who'll make the difference if we just go along;
So teach us dependence and with Your banner unfurled,
We'll battle on our knees, and we will light the world!

Stargazer

Out on a hill in the stillness of night
My eyes fix upon some far point of light
Deep in the vastness of space.
Cool breezes gently brush against my cheek
And I know it's not some star that I seek
But He, who hung it in place.

Oh, what could bring more appreciation
For the wonder of Your creation
Than the beauty of a starlit sky.
Your power is beyond comprehension
And I am required to give attention
To Your glory revealed on high.

For alone on that hill, I know Your will,
Is for me to stand here grateful and still,
Knowing Who made all I see.
Oh, Father of Lights, when I'm stargazing
I must admit what I find most amazing
Is the grace that you've given to me.

It brings my soul joy beyond all measure
To know You've chosen as your own treasure
This fragile vessel of clay.
You made and placed each galaxy and star
But chose the heart of this earthen jar
To fill with Yourself every day.

A Call to Persevere

One winter morning, I woke up to see the trees surrounding my home looking beautiful with heavy snow hanging on the branches and the ground totally covered in unblemished white. Perfection! However, underneath that perfect blanket of snow was a lot of imperfection. It became quite evident the next day when two of my granddaughters, Abby and Micaiah, went out to build snowmen. They had a fantastic time, and the snowmen were a lot of fun. But it was interesting that as they rolled the huge balls of snow a lot of things that had been hidden became visible. The balls had leaves and twigs and dead grass sticking in them. The blanket of snow had disguised all that imperfection. All of our lives are full of imperfection and we spend a great deal of time and energy trying to cover it up or get rid of it completely, but we never really can. Our flaws are there because we are not perfect. Far from it, we are born into this world with a sin nature.

There are days—more days than we like to admit—when because we have that sin nature, we disappoint ourselves. Sometimes our bad behavior is evident to the people around us. At other times they may not be at all aware, because our outward behavior can appear just fine like that pristine snow-covered grass. But, in our inmost being we are aware of what others may not see. We know our thoughts and our attitudes. We know when we serve others without a servant's heart or have a lack of gratitude or selfish motives. What others cannot see, God does. He gently draws our attention to these inner failings. When we see them for ourselves, as Christians, we can feel such sorrow over our sin and such a strong desire to be more like Jesus.

I wrote the poem "More Like You" when my heart was filled with sorrow over my own attitude and I had poured out my confession to the Lord asking his forgiveness. It's always amazing to me that when I do turn to the Lord in repentance, what I feel is all His love and encouragement. In this life, we will continue to have those disappointing days. The Christian life is a journey and on that journey we are being transformed, but that transformation will not be complete until we are home in heaven. When that day arrives, we will finally be free from our old nature, from the presence of sin and we will forever be more like Him.

More Like You

Lord, when am I going to be more like You?
I constantly do what I don't want to do.
And when will I learn, Lord, to do things Your way?
I've failed You again, like a sheep gone astray.

You call to me, Lord, and I do hear Your voice.
And You point out again that I've made the wrong choice.
You carry me back, set my feet on Your path.
I feel all Your love. I deserve all Your wrath.

The longer I serve You, the brighter Your light.
You illumine my heart. It's black, Lord, not white.
I don't want to fail You. I love You, my King.
I wanted today to You glory to bring.

Lord, when am I going to be more like You,
And not sin in things that I think, say, or do?
And when will I bridle this quick-speaking tongue
From which careless words are so hastily flung?

O how I long to obey all Your commands,
To only sing praises, lift up holy hands.
I do love You, Lord, O, I honestly do,
So when am I going to be more like You?

Yes, I know You've changed me from who I have been.

It just grieves my heart to have failed You again.

I feel Your forgiveness and hope springs anew.

There will be a day when I will be like You.

And on that sweet day I will stand at Your side

As part of Your body, Your church, and Your bride.

And never again will I fail to be true.

In heaven You'll make me forever like You.

Glimpses of Glory

I hope you didn't miss it; oh, so swiftly did it fly
That single special moment when we all were lifted high
And we could see so clearly the bright glory of His grace
Revealed for that one instant in the peace upon her face

Brief glimpses of His glory at the lifting of the veil
That moment when God's great power was able to prevail
Against all that seems normal to the doubters of this place
A heart that could have filled with fear was guarded by His grace

Because she made a choice, and you can choose to make it, too
The choice to trust and praise the Lord in all that's sent to you
The good, the bad, the joy, the pain; just face it all the same
With the kind of trusting faith that brings glory to His name

Remember in Zephaniah's book, where the prophet writes
About how over his children the Lord, himself delights
Well, I think that this trusting, faithful daughter of the King
Must have caused her heavenly Father to rejoice and sing

Go give glimpses of His glory to other weary souls
For I know you'll want to do that, if loving God's your goal
For all that we can offer Him is the gift we watched her give
The gift of showing others how He wants for them to live

Sheltered in the Shadow

Lord, shelter me beneath Your wings
For in their shadow my soul sings
Protected there, secure and warm
I'm filled with joy and kept from harm

Your perfect love casts out all fear
And I am safe. You draw me near
Though I may lose my worldly wealth
Though disease my strip away my health

Nothing should strike my soul with fear
No one can take what I hold dear
Your love for me is guaranteed
And more than that I should not need

Beneath the shadow of Your wings
It won't matter what this life brings
Just keep me constantly aware
Of your presence; You're always there

Open my spiritual eyes to see
The wings that overshadow me
Then no matter what comes along
I'll have the faith to finish strong

Sailing through the Storm

based on sermon notes from an Adrian Rogers broadcast 4/2/2000

Grounded by His providence, guarded by His power
I know that I can trust Him in this my darkest hour
For He knew all my needs back before the dawn of time
And I know that His own hand is tightly holding mine

Graced by His sweet prayers and growing by His own plan
Though I may not feel like it, I know that I can stand
For I am safely held in those everlasting arms
And though the storm is raging, He will keep me from harm

Gladdened by His presence for He's with me everywhere
There's nothing for one to fear who's safely in His care
Wherever His will leads me, I can securely go
Knowing His grace will keep me. His word says that it's so.

Guided by His purpose even when it isn't clear
He works things out for my good, I don't have to fear
Though smooth sailing isn't promised for my life's little ship
I will reach the final destination of this trip

Making Music in Your Heart

Do you know how you can make your own heart sing,
No matter what trials you see this life bring
Can you be content with what may come along,
Still hearing the song in your heart playing strong

Can you still be thankful when things fall apart,
And keep singing God's praise from the depths of your heart?
Or are all your emotions controlling your day?
Do your feelings decide what you think and say?

Do you live for yourself or for the Lord's glory?
Is trusting in Him the real theme of your story?
For if God's at the center, the music will play,
No matter what circumstances enter your day.

So just yield to the Spirit; be filled and be free
To become the person you know you want to be
With joy that is steady and hope that is strong
And a heart that keeps playing the notes of God's song

Facing the Giant

Men stood and shouted the battle cry that day
But when they saw the giant they ran away
So afraid that they would die
But young David's heart knew no such dread and fear
For to the heart of God, he had drawn so near
On God's name he could rely

So undaunted by Goliath's threats and jeers
And then ignoring everyone else's fears
He prepared to face his foe
He chose five smooth stones and a simple sling
Those weren't the only weapons he had to bring
In the name of God he'd go

The most amazing thing about this well-known tale
Isn't that David's battle plans didn't fail
But that he carried them through
That his faith in God was so incredibly strong
That he used those weapons he brought along
In the name of the God he knew

So I thought about the giants I face now
One's I've sought to defeat but haven't known how
And prepared to face each foe
What five stones would I carefully choose to bring?
What powerful weapons should hurl from my sling?
When in God's great name I go

I asked the Lord to help me choose these five
Weapons for war that will help me to survive
On the spiritual battlefield
First I had to choose confession of sin
For without a clean heart, I could never win
My stubborn pride had to yield

The next weapon was God's wonderful word
All those biblical truths that I've read and heard
And have hidden in my heart
Another great weapon I know I must raise
Is the powerful weapon of songs of praise
I felt almost ready to start

I had chosen three weapons and needed two
And then God reminded me about you
The support of Christian love
And then one more weapon I chose as my last
For there may be times when I'll need to fast
To focus on God above

But selecting weapons is not enough
The next step is what will be really tough
I can't just prepare a plan
Without more delay I must descend the hill
To the giant who waits to see if I will
And in Jesus' name I can

Choosing Hope

Sometimes my road is a rocky one
And clouds of gloom seem to block the sun
On my saddest darkest days
When streams of trials will not halt
Still in the Lord, Himself, I will exalt
And give Him all my praise

For I know His hand is holding mine
And I'll make it through and be just fine
He'll never let me fall
I know that I will persevere
As his purchased child I have no fear
He'll always hear me call

And if I go forward and don't complain
About all the sorrow and the pain
And keep a thankful heart
Then proven character will surely be
What God will bring about in me
He planned that from the start

And my trust and hope in Him will grow

As trials teach me what I need to know

About the Lord above

Who pours His own love into my soul

Heals my broken heart and makes me whole

A channel for His love

For that is what trials should really do

As they come to me and they come to you

Make vessels God can use

To bring His love to all mankind

To the broken hearted and the blind

When hope is what we choose

Trusting God

Lord, I know that I must trust You
Even when I can't understand
Why the hardships that I walk through
Serve some purpose that you planned

Oh, it's easier to do so
To trust your answers when I pray
When problems quickly come and go
Than when some problems come and stay

When rocky paths are not so long
And perhaps there's an end in sight
Then faith and hope can seem so strong
And all my burdens seem so light

But when some problems still remain
When I have prayed over them for years
My heart grows weary with the strain
And in my weakness I feel fears

Yet, still your sweet Spirit tells me
I must remind my weary soul
That an end to hardship must not be
My life's real purpose or real goal

My heart's goal must be to love You
To be empowered by your hand
To praise and trust and honor You
No matter what you've planned

And so dear Lord, I come to You
Not to seek an end to strife
But to seek for strength in all I do
To bring You glory through my life

Hold Me Gently

Hold me gently, Father. I feel so much alone.
I need the grace and mercy, You have always shown.
Fill my cup completely until it overflows.
How desperately I need You, only heaven knows.

Hold me gently, Father. Draw me close to You;
Even though I fail you in what I say and do.
Your love, grace and mercy, I never understand,
But I know that no one can snatch me from Your hand.

And that includes myself. Yes, nothing I can do,
Will ever change the fact that I belong to You.
No matter if I've fallen into Satan's snare.
You will come to rescue. You never cease to care.

All that I must do is confess to You my sin,
Then turning from my failure, once more I'll begin.
And I'll rise up in faith to face another day
Grateful that You've taught me to turn to You and pray.

Hold me gently, Father. I'm weary from the fight.
Before I face another day, protect me with Your might.
Wrap me up in arms of love. Wipe away my tears.
Give me courage. Give me strength. Take away my fears.

My heart is ever grateful for all that You have done.

You placed the penalty for my sin on Your only Son.

And so this wounded soldier; this needy, broken soul

Through Your mercy and Your grace is again made whole.

From the Snare of the Fowler

In this sleepless night hear my distress filled plea
As I search Your Word seeking to be set free
From the snare of the fowler hear my soul's groans
A broken spirit is drying up my bones

Fighting the darkness and the liar's powers
I wrestle despair in the night's lonely hours
The enemy taunts me that You'll hide Your face
He speaks of my weakness but not of Your grace

You hear my tormented soul silently scream
From the depths of this pit, my life You'll redeem
With love and compassion, my head You will crown
I will rise up again. I will not stay down

For great is Your love. You're righteous and just
And in Your mercy and strength I always will trust
To all Your promises I fervently cling
You'll satisfy my desires with Your good things

I know I'm a vapor, mere dust from the earth
Yet because of Your love I know I have worth
The Prince of darkness must flee from this place
For when I cry for help, You don't hide Your face

A Call to the
Spiritual Disciplines

Many years ago, I walked through a season in my life filled with sorrow and incredible disappointment and stress. It was hard for me to sleep at night, and my thoughts were flooded with worry. At that time I happened to be reading Philippians 4:8, a passage which admonishes us to think about things that are true, noble, right, pure, lovely, admirable, excellent or praiseworthy. I cried out to God telling Him how difficult it was for me to be able to do that. I felt Him speak to my heart that His Word certainly was all of those things, and that I needed to fill my thoughts with Scripture. I began that day to memorize the book of James. I spent countless hours committing it to memory and discovered an amazing benefit in so doing. At night when my mind wanted to fret about problems, I would lie in bed and go over as many chapters as it took for me to drift off into a peaceful sleep.

When I finished memorizing James, I continued with more books of the Bible. The Bible became more precious to me than ever before. I gained a much deeper understanding of God's Word than I had ever known from isolated Scriptures. My relationship with the Lord grew sweeter and I changed in my ability to trust Him in difficult circumstances. Many people tell me that they could not memorize this way, but I suggest that they spend great amounts of time meditating on God's Word. I usually memorize about 4 chapters of the Bible in a year. I think if most Christians would meditate on the same 4 chapters each day for a year, they might just be surprised at how much of it they could commit to memory. But, whether or not they were able to memorize those verses, I know that they would in some form be written on their hearts. Give it a try. You may just be blessed by the practice.

The poem "Until the Morning Star Rises" is my prayer that God would continue to deepen my love for His Word. I know that I must be totally dependent on Him. I know my own weakness and His strength. The phrase "until the morning star rises" comes from 2 Peter 1:19.

And we have the word of the prophets made more certain,
and you will do well to pay attention to it,
as to a light shining in a dark place, until the day dawns
and the morning star rises in your hearts.
2 Peter 1:19 NIV

Until the Morning Star Rises

Oh, Father, help me love your word
With greater passion every day
Always seeing it as the light
That shines to guide me on my way

Never let the fire within me
Burn to ashes, cold and dry
Write your commands upon my heart
'Til your word makes my spirit fly

And keep me forever faithful
I, who have feeble, faithless ways
And deliver me from evil
Touch my lips to bring forth praise

Until the last day dawns and the
Morning star rises within me
May I be a doer of your word
Not one who hears forgetfully

The Privilege of Prayer

Lord, wake me each day with praise on my tongue.

Place on my lips a beautiful song to be sung.

When morning breaks forth, may I at first be aware,

Of my need to start with the privilege of prayer.

As the day rushes on with the business of life,

May I draw apart from the clamor and strife,

And in quiet moments come to that special place,

Where I turn once again to the Giver of Grace.

O God, my dear Father, at each long day's end.

Cause me to remember that these knees need to bend,

And offering thanks with a heart full of love,

Send the fragrance of prayer into heaven above.

Grateful Hearts

Lord, I saw her last night, this girl just eleven
Her mother is with You now up there in heaven.
And the child is alone in a Pakistani town,
Since You've given her dear mother the martyr's crown.

Tears streamed down her face as she cooked her meal.
It was hard to watch pain and suffering so real.
She wept for the mother who is no longer there,
But she didn't complain or shout, "It's not fair!"

Nor has she stopped putting her trust in You.
You are still Lord and her heart is still true.
Then I thought of the glory she brings to Your name,
And honestly, Father, it made me feel shame.

Oh Lord, forgive me for my selfish attitude
When my own prayers are not filled with gratitude.
I've been called a Christian for many a year
And for wearing Your name I have never known fear.

Lord, let all Christians living in this blessed land
Remember how gently we've been held in Your hand.
And then help us all to freely serve and to give
Thankful each day for the place where You've let us live!

He Knows

He knows. He knows my innermost thoughts
All that I've learned; all that I've been taught
And all the lessons I've yet to learn,
All the truths that I do not discern

He knows my each and every need
He sees each good and each evil deed
And everything I will say is heard
Before I begin to utter a word

Nothing can ever be done by me
That my dear Father did not foresee
It brings me peace and joy just to know
That He loves me though He knows me so

So when I fail I don't have to hide
All my sins and weaknesses I confide
In the One by Whom they are already known
And to me has always mercy shown

So don't be afraid to let Him start
To correct your faults and change your heart
Don't be ashamed. Be grateful instead
Be filled with eagerness not with dread

For the Lord of Life, the great I Am
Is willing to teach one straying lamb
Accept His grace and His discipline, too
He gives them both out of love for you

Considering it All Joy

I've heard many an eloquent preacher preach.
And I've watched many a gifted teacher teach.
Many are the offerings I've seen men bring.
So many great singers, I've heard sweetly sing.

But those who show me most that God's truly there
Are those who smile though they have burdens to bear.
As I look at those faces lit up with a smile,
I know they count as joy each and every trial.

In them the power of Jesus Christ is plain,
As they rise above their particular pain.
They glorify God and lift up their brothers.
Their testimonies are above all others.

A Call to the
Fruit of the Spirit

As believers, we want to see the fruit of the Spirit produced in our lives, but we learn that spiritual fruit grows slowly. It comes as we walk through the trials of life and find that God is there. We learn to trust, and the suffering we go through leads to perseverance. When we learn to persevere through it all we develop character—character that exhibits love, joy, peace, patience, kindness, goodness, faithfulness, gentleness and self-control. All the fruit of the Spirit begins to become evident in our lives.

Going through trials is never a pleasant experience, but as believers, we learn that we can consider it all joy as the first chapter of James tells us. It is true that we grow closer to Christ and mature more in times of trial than we do at any other time. God uniquely uses these times in our lives to grow our faith, renew our minds and change our hearts. The truth of Scripture becomes more evident to us, and bit by bit, we mature in our understanding of who God is. Trust deepens and we continue to have greater hope as God pours out his love into our hearts.

In the poem, "Harvest of Hope," I have expressed the hope and trust I have in God as a result of all the trials I have passed through. I have always found Him faithful, and I know I always will.

Not only so, but we also rejoice in our sufferings,
because we know that suffering produces perseverance;
perseverance, character; and character, hope.
Romans 5:3-4 NIV

Harvest of Hope

As the farmer waits for the fruit of his toil,
For precious produce to break forth from the soil,
So my own desert dry soul sometimes must wait
For spiritual fruit grows at its own slow rate

But one thing I've discovered, one thing I know
Is that fruit of the spirit will surely grow
Though it may be watered by tender tears
As God teaches me to overcome my fears

And to count as joy every trial and test
Knowing in His time I will truly be blessed
For seeds of faith I've sown will mature one day
In my own heart, if I'll persevere and pray

And if I'll truly take the Lord at His word,
Believing all the scriptures I've heard
If I still trust God at the end of my rope
I will reap one day the great harvest of hope

Hearts at Peace

Our hectic lives now appear so full of care,
That a heart found at peace may seem all too rare.
In a world that moves on at a breakneck pace,
We're running for our lives in the human race.

And as we run, we choose to fret and worry.
What else do you do when you're in such a hurry?
As we worry we can miss all of life's best
Because we fail in giving God our requests.

Leaving all our fears and anxieties there,
We are to trust in Him at the end of each prayer,
And with thanksgiving accept His release,
With hearts that are guarded by His perfect peace.

And then setting our minds on that which is good,
We'll choose to live by faith as we know we should.
When worries seek into our thoughts to pour,
We'll lock them all out and not open the door.

Empty Vessels

Just as the widow in Elisha's day
Was faced with debt impossible to pay
So we come to our God as paupers, too
Beggars needing what He alone can do

As Elisha sent her to shut the door
And to trust the Lord for the oil she'd pour
So behind closed doors, Jesus sends us to pray
And to trust our God in much the same way

Not for oil that we can hold in a jar
But for oil that's more valuable by far
For the vessel He wants us to lift up
Is our heart's empty spiritual cup

A cup cleansed by repentance of our sin
Ready for his Holy Spirit to flow in
Each vessel she gathered was filled that day
And God wants to fill us in the same way

And though the widow filled one final cup
Our God will never cease to fill us up
Again and again we can shut our door
And down on our knees, we can ask for more

Then rivers of blessing will flow our way
When in a secret place, we stop to pray
For we who entered the room spiritually poor
Can be rich as kings when we open the door

Guaranteed Joy

Joy is your birthright, my dear Christian friend
So walk in that joy from now to the end
Oh yes count it all joy, you've cause for elation
For yours is the joy of God's great salvation

Joy that remains through trials and tears
And helps overcome all of your fears
Joy that erupts with laughter and smiles
Even when facing those seasons of trials

Joy that depends on God's work in your heart
Confessing and receiving is your only part
Joy that's unshaken, that does not depend
On the blessings God may or may not choose to send

Joy that is rooted and grounded in love
Not love we give, but love sent from above
Joy like a magnet that draws broken souls
To the One who can make broken lives whole

Count it your joy, my dear sisters and friends
As the journey of life takes its twists and its bends
God gives you such joy and it makes you strong
For joy is God singing your heart a love song

Growing in Grace

O dear child of God, I wonder if you know

That He rejoices over you as you grow

Though He knows you've far to go

And He understands all the struggle and strain

He is very pleased with every tiny gain

Just because He loves you so

He wants for you to become mature and strong

But He knows that the process is slow and long

And filled with painful choices

Even though you stumble and make mistakes

He knows the courage repentance takes

And o'er broken hearts rejoices

You're the treasure of the Great Heavenly King

The precious child that makes Him smile and sing

He wants you to know He cares

Don't let your failures start getting you down

Or trade in your smiles for the enemy's frown

Your Father hears all your prayers

He wants for you to give Him your love, too

And to enjoy the freedom He bought for you

So believe His truth, not lies

Don't ever live in shame or in fear or dread

Just trust your Father's love and relax instead

You're His beloved child who tries

River of Peace

The river of peace starts out as a stream
It's so softly flowing that it may seem
Not like a river at all
But the One who sends the wind and the rain
Knows the power the little stream will gain
As the rains begin to fall

Toward the eternal sea the river flows
Through the twists and bends of life it goes
Growing deeper every day
The deepening river is flowing on
And then so suddenly the rains are gone
And a drought has come its way

The sun beats down as the river dries
Through all the questions, and through all the whys
Now the slowing stream must wait
Then in His time and for His own reasons
The Lord God will bring the rainy season
At ever increasing rate

Suddenly a raging flood is rising
And its coming may be so surprising
To all but the Lord above
For He alone knew that this time was planned
When mercifully He'd reach out His hand
And pour out His rain of love

So the river of peace continues to flow
As all of life's droughts and floods come and go
It becomes a mighty force
'Til flowing out to the eternal sea
It reaches its God-given destiny
Because the stream stayed its course

Just for Today

James explained how we can receive
Wisdom from our God if we'll just believe
And then trust Him to provide
We must ask in faith if we are able
To be secure and completely stable
And put all our doubts aside

We ask our glorious Father to give
Wisdom and revelation as we live
So we may know Him better
That's what Paul said that he continued to pray
For the church that he wrote to on that day
In his long Ephesians letter

So when I needed wisdom from God this week
I asked and then waited for Him to speak
Eager for what He would say
For I was weary and needed to know
How to withstand stress that just won't go
So He said, just for today

Just for today obey all my commands
Remember you are upheld by my hand
You know I will see you through
Just for today give Me all your love
Just for today keep your eyes above
I'll be there in all you do

So just don't try to live by months and years

You'll be exhausted and so full of fears

You must live just for today

I know that you've already found this true

It's not the first time I've reminded you

That this is the only way

Always There

Thank you, Abba Father for holding me up
And for filling so completely my once empty cup
For courage to trust You and to truly believe
For teaching me life is a tapestry You weave

For peace in the midst of this trial in my life
That stabs at my heart like the blade of a knife
For healing that pain and for restoring my soul
For returning the joy that Satan thought he stole

For giving me the wisdom to know what to do
And for focusing my eyes and my thoughts on You
For showing me that apart from Your might and power
I couldn't stand firm for even one single hour

Yes, I thank You the most, Lord, for letting me know
That I'd fall apart if You ever let me go
I've no hope, joy, strength, not a particle of peace
Unless I trust that my hand You won't release

But you've made me a promise I know You will keep
So in the midst of the storm I drift off to sleep
Knowing Abba, Father, that You will always care
And no matter what life brings, You always will be there

From Glory to Glory

a response to a Living Proof seminar, Memphis, TN, June 8-9, 2001

Teach me, O Lord, what I cannot know

So from glory to glory I can go

Forgive me for all my unbelief

For my faithlessness that has caused you grief

And never cease to work on me

Until I've been healed and have broken free

Let me repent and renounce my wrong

So my soul can sing you a pure love song

Change my heart, motivation and sight

So I see others in your loving light

And let them see me with unveiled face

As one who desperately needs your grace

Let me give you time I need to give

As you patiently teach me how to live

And when I can't see all you've planned

Help me trust you until you lift your hand

But most of all, Sweet Servant King

Let me be bathed by the deep love you bring

So your selfless love will overflow

From my changed heart wherever I go

A Call to Serve

I love studying and I always have. I loved the beginning of a new school year both as a student and later as a teacher. I retired from teaching mathematics, but Bible studies are still a passion of mine. Studying the Word and understanding more of the amazing truth of the Bible intrigues me, and the start of each new study fills me with expectation. Many of you are probably just like me. You genuinely love learning and can spend countless hours reading and reflecting on what you learn. You love to spend hours discussing all you've learned with friends.

I also love music. It stirs my heart and soul. Sunday mornings joining my voice with others praising the Lord brings deep joy. I love joyful choruses and the deep, reflective hymns of the past. There are times my hands are raised in praise and times when I want to kneel before the Lord. Most Christians seem to deeply enjoy worship just as I do.

One morning I was reading John 13 and came to the 17th verse where after Jesus had washed the disciples' feet, He says, "Now that you know these things you will be blessed if you do them." Suddenly, I thought, are we the church, the body of Christ, doing what we know? We need to study the Word, we need to fellowship together, and we need to worship the Lord together. All of those things are wonderful, but sometimes I wondered, do we fail to humbly serve those around us as Jesus modeled for us? Are we lowering ourselves to serve as He did as He washed the disciples' feet? We all know so much about what we need to do, and yet sometimes we fail to do it. Jesus tells us that we will be blessed in doing not simply in knowing.

My thoughts that morning resulted in the poem I called "Now That You Know." When I read it, it reminds me to be sure that I don't get so caught up in learning about Christ that I fail to model Him in humble service to those around me. Our communities need to see Christ in action in us.

Now that you know these things,
you will be blessed if you do them.

John 13:17 NIV

Now That You Know

Now that you know, yes, now that you've heard
Now that you've read and you've studied God's word
What are you going to do?
Now that He's told you of His great love
And promised a place in His kingdom above
A place prepared just for you

Now that you've studied for hours or years
Now that you know you have nothing to fear
What are you going to do?
Now that you've sung all those pretty praise songs
And proclaimed your faith is where it belongs
Is His light shining through you?

Are you humbly serving all you know
And letting Christ lead wherever you go
No matter what lies ahead?
Now that you know the last shall be first
Now that He's fed you and quenched your thirst
Are you doing what He said?

Are you still waiting as life goes by
Like a bird that's refusing to fly
Not putting wings to the test
Servant, it's time to serve; you must go
Remember Christ said, now that you know
It's in doing that you'll be blessed

Full Notebooks or Full Hearts?

Our notebooks are full. We've studied the Word.
And countless are the sermons we've heard.
Retreats and conferences fill our days.
We're moved to tears by songs of praise.

We know the words. We can talk the talk.
But why don't we learn to walk the walk.
We cry out to You for our survival.
Please send Your people a true revival.

Bring in our hearts absolute surrender.
Forgive each brokenhearted offender.
On this day, Father, and in this hour
We need Your Holy Spirit's power.

Open up spiritually blinded eyes.
Don't just give us head knowledge; make us wise.
Fan the flame into fire within each soul.
Make loving You our one and only goal.

Bondslaves of Christ?

We are saved by faith but not to sit.
That's a fact we often don't admit.
Bondslaves of Christ, pretending we're free.
"Jesus calls others to serve, not me!"

That spiritual gift is not mine.
I'll stay on the sofa and recline.
Someone is needed more skilled than I.
Do we really believe that old lie?

I think we know it's ingratitude
That is the root of our attitude.
Remember the price He paid for you,
And start to ask Him what you can do!

Dependence

Before I even begin to pray
Remind me that I'm just a lump of clay.
Let me not hold up my own design.
That's the Potter's job and never mine.

Don't let me give You a plan to bless.
What's best for me I can't even guess.
You, my dear Father, are the only one,
Who should direct each daughter or son.

What if You did give me my own way?
I might miss the joy You'd planned today.
And what is worse, I might never grow
To learn Your ways or Your truth to know.

No, let me ask that Your will be done,
From when I rise to the setting sun.
Let me ask for this; to hear Your voice.
Make obeying You my only choice.

Left on my own, I will always fail,
But following You, through rough seas sail,
For You will keep me from Satan's harm,
As an eagle I'll soar above life's storm.

Rapture

It is so easy our attention to capture
Just ask our opinion on the upcoming Rapture.
We have pre-trip, mid-trib, and post-trib positions.
We just don't agree on expected conditions.

It's easy for us to get caught up in debate
On whether He'll return very early or late.
But whether we are wrong or whether we are right,
He's still going to come like a thief in the night.

I doubt if He will care what opinion we hold.
I know that He cares how many people we've told.
Opinions are harmless and interesting to share,
But let's try to help others meet Him in the air.

A Call to
Intimacy with Christ

None of us get to go through life without encountering trouble. We all experience disappointment, fear, sorrow and grief. Learning to cast our cares on the Lord is so important. We have to learn who God is and how we can trust Him to be there whatever we are going through. We learn to know God best as we study and meditate on His word.

One of my favorite Scripture passages is Psalm 91. It speaks of God's protective nature. When we are fearful, we can trade all of our fears for trust in the God who loves us. He is our refuge and our fortress. When we choose to trust the Lord in the midst of our troubles, He gives us His peace. I love the image of being covered by His wings just as a mother hen protectively covers her chicks. Focusing on the Father's loving protective nature brings comfort in the midst of sorrow.

My husband Al and I both find great comfort in memorizing and meditating on Scripture. Some time ago, Al was memorizing Psalm 91 and going over those verses as he went about some outdoor work. He had decided to cut a dead branch from the oak tree in our yard. The branch was about 20 feet off the ground and Al climbed up his extension ladder chainsaw in hand. As he started to saw off the branch his ladder slipped and flipped over so that Al was falling from the back of the ladder. He said he was sure he was going to die that day. Suddenly, the ladder hit another branch and stopped. Al was able to hang on and climb down the ladder from the back, rescued from a seemingly impossible situation. He immediately thanked God for His protective care and for the blessing of living to see another day.

When I face life's difficult moments I often turn to Psalm 91 and for Al these verses are especially sweet. The poem, "In the Shadow," is one of the poems I have written based on the truths of this beautiful psalm.

"He will cover you with His feathers, and
under His wings you will find refuge;
His faithfulness will be your shield and rampart."

Psalm 91:4 NIV

In the Shadow

Rest in the shadow of the Lord Almighty
Covered by his feathers so protectively
Faithfully seek and find your refuge there
Under his wings, within his tender care

Where you can forget about the sorrow this world brings
And listen to the new song your own heart sings
In the shadow; in the shadow of his wings

Quietly now let your tired spirit yield
To the one whose faithfulness is your shield
All life brings your way you can safely face
If you make the Most High your dwelling place

Where no enemy can harm you or cause you grief
Relax in his love with trust and true belief
In the shadow; in the shadow find relief

Acknowledge his name and be protected there
Rescued and saved from the fowler's snare
You've nothing to fear by day or by night
No matter what battles you have to fight

All attacks against you will have to cease
For his angels on your behalf he will release
In the shadow; in the shadow all is peace

The Secret Place

What drives me to the secret place
Is not the life of ease
It is the hurdles in this race
That brings me to my knees

At times when the road is steepest
When trials seem so long
My longing is the deepest
For Abba's arms so strong

And it is in the secret place
The precious prayerful hour
Of seeking and of finding grace
That I receive power

Not power that will end all pain
My sorrows I'll still grieve
But in the secret place I gain
The power to believe

And when the trials finally end
When brighter days I face
Then a grateful heart still will send
Me to that secret place

Hearing the Wind

Dry leaves are lifted and blown on the ground

By unseen winds with a howling sound

And though I can't see such currents of air

The howling wind assures me that it's there

Like invisible winds I know are real

By the sounds I hear and the breeze I feel

I cannot see that the Lord God is there

And so I offer up to Him my prayer

Lord, let me hear Your voice with my soul's ears

So that I feel Your love and know You're near

As the wind of Your Spirit lifts away

Every burden of care I had today

Breathing His Name

In all the sorrow I feel today
I still find peace when I stop and pray
And put all my trust in my King
Though my heart's heavy with care and grief
In the arms of Christ there is relief
And my spirit still can sing

For I know that I'm never alone
He hears each breath, each cry and each moan
He shares all my heartache and pain
From depths of my soul I breathe His name
Jesus, Jesus, He's always the same
And His comfort soothes me again

At His Father's side, He breathes my name
Praying for me, forever the same
My Savior, my Lord and my friend
So I know that I will make it through
He'll stay with me whatever I do
He will be faithful 'til the end

On the Best or Worst of Days

All my soul has ever needed, all for which I've ever pleaded
All the hungers of a famished heart
Every wound in need of healing, all the stress with which I'm dealing
Every blow that's torn my world apart

You remove all the aching from my burdened back that's breaking
and fill the empty places in my soul
You dry my tears as they're falling when I hear your sweet voice calling
You make my heart's ragged fragments whole

All you ask is that I trust you and have faith in what you will do
Believing every promise you have made
I know it's true that you love me; good things come from above me
As your mercy once more is displayed

So, Father, I will sing your praise on the best or worst of days
I know there can be no other way
I have lived long enough now that I think I may have learned how
To recognize my need to stop and pray

Self Analysis

One of the most difficult battles ever fought
Is to unlearn lessons carefully taught.
Do you analyze with great devotion
The source of unexpected emotion?

Perhaps our studies of psychology
Are now affecting our theology.
Modern man finds it most appealing
To seek out the root of every feeling.

But as we look deeply within for the source,
We're embarking on a dangerous course.
The deeper we probe, the deeper we delve,
The more all our focus is on ourselves.

When Satan attacks instead of resisting,
We often find ourselves assisting.
Though as Christians, we're by God empowered,
We can allow ourselves to be devoured.

It is hard for us to understand,
When we feel or act in a way unplanned.
We want to be giving, to really have cared,
Not to be jealous or angry or scared.

So when we are what we don't want to be,

We make quite a target for our enemy.

Though we're all different, we're much the same.

When we don't like ourselves, we seek to blame.

It's my sad childhood, my husband, my wife,

My children, or the disappointment of life,

My neighbors, my employer, the church we attend,

Someone or something caused me to offend.

But we know that's not true, it isn't so!

If we want to change, to God we must go.

He'll change our feelings and our behavior,

He knows our need. That's why He's our Savior.

Purchased Privilege

Lord, my heart is heavy and it's weighted down with fear
I don't feel your presence yet I know that You are near
My eyes are on my problems and thoughts of what might be
I must resist the devil. Your truth will make him flee

I'm bringing You this burden. I'll place it at your feet
Forcing my adversary to make a quick retreat
For when I pray quickly, I'm quickly filled with peace
And any grasp he has on me, he quickly must release

Though he battles for my heart and wants to take each thought
He can't have the victory; my freedom has been bought
Thank You once again for the price You chose to pay
To buy for me the privilege that is mine when I pray

The privilege of position as daughter of the King
I can approach the throne of God asking anything
And know that my Father will always hear each plea
Your answers, Lord, will always be just what is best for me

You may not remove my problems, at least not right away
But You will give me power and strength to live another day
And since You'll be beside me walking with me everywhere
You'll assure me that the burden's light enough to bear

Reflections at Sunrise

In the stillness of the morning, as the sun begins to rise
And glimpses of soft sunlight fall on my expectant eyes
My heart is full of praises for my Lord, the King of Kings
And deep down within my spirit, my heart and soul sings

For I have met this new day reflecting on His sweet love
And all the grace and mercy that He pours out from above
To one who is unworthy, one deserving loss and pain
And who instead of loss has now been given such great gain

For His compassion fails not; oh, His mercy's always new
And He is ever patient and so kind to me and you
So now I stand and glorify the Giver of all light
Who turns mourning into dancing and
brings daylight forth from night

Lord, I am so grateful for the forgiveness I receive
Let my life reflect gratitude and all that I believe
For You are the greatest treasure that I will ever find
Help me truly love You with all my heart and soul and mind

Secret of Satisfaction

If I could have the finest home great wealth could buy
And have fine clothes and jewels all in vast supply
Oh, if I could have all things
And travel all the world; see all there is to see
Dine as kings have dined and eat just what pleases me
Have the best that this world brings

If I could hear applause; be flattered by men's praise
Be given power to control all my life's days
If I could have my own way
Life would still be empty unless I heard Your voice
For if I'm choosing treasure, You must be my choice
Lord, I must hear what You say

Nothing this world offers can fill my hungry soul
No earthly wealth will ever make my spirit whole
Only You can satisfy
For I've tasted and I've found that the Lord is good
I've found in Jesus Christ all that I hoped I would
And I'll tell the whole world why

It's because there's nothing else that can bring His peace
Feed my soul, quench my thirst and make my struggles cease
Nothing else with ever do
So what I want to tell each seeker I'm around
Is that all that matters is this secret I've found
It's not what you have but Who

A Call to Finish Well

I think most Christians have a deep desire to please the Lord, and I think most Christians are also very aware of their own failures and flaws. We know ourselves, and we are know how easy it is to do the things we don't want to do. The longer we walk with the Lord the more He sheds light on our hearts. We become more and more aware of how much we need to depend on the Lord. The deeper our love for the Lord becomes, the more we want to please Him, and the more we know that doing that requires Him to transform us from the inside out. Our prayers are for Him to work in us and through us and to work out His will in our lives.

Each time we attempt to do things in our own strength, we get the opportunity to taste failure. We aren't always aware of our own self-reliance until God reveals it to us. The beauty of our relationship with Christ is that our weaknesses never surprise Him, only us. And our failures never diminish His love for us. He lets us learn from our mistakes, and encourages our hearts as we walk with Him. Our relationship with the Lord deepens and we renew our hope in Him.

As believer's we look forward to being with the Lord one day, and we want to hear Him say that He knew we loved Him as we walked on earth. We long to hear the words, well done, from the Lord. I thought about this one day, and wrote the poem, "Life's Prize." I long to hear that "well done" at the end of my journey, and I am so aware that the only way that will happen is through the transforming work of the Holy Spirit in me.

His master replied, 'Well done, good and faithful servant!
You have been faithful with a few things;
I will put you in charge of many things.
Come and share your master's happiness!'
Matthew 25:23 NIV

Life's Prize

Lord, I long to hear what I want You to say
When I stand in Your presence on the first day
That my eyes can behold Your glory
I want You to tell me that You knew I loved You
That You found within me a heart that was true
Make my life reflect that love story

For You have filled me up with such strong desires
That my heart ever yearns and longs and aspires
To be filled with a fullness that's new
For I have only begun to taste and to see
All that You have planned and have in store for me
When my heart is surrendered to You

When submission's normal as drawing a breath
And Your life flows out from the crucified death
Oh, when I cease to be in control
When I love You more than I ever loved me
And my prayers consist of that one heartfelt plea
That Your will becomes my only goal

Perfect devotion's something I cannot give
I know I will fall short as long as I live
But help me love You better today
So that in heaven my life's prize will be won
By hearing You say to me, "Servant, well done!"
Let me hear those sweet words, I pray

Run 'Til the Race is Through

Are there days when your Bible stays on the shelf;
Days when you can't seem to encourage yourself;
Days when God seems far away?
Are there times when negative emotions
Keep you from enjoying daily devotions;
Times when you don't want to pray?

Those times when you don't think you'll finish the race,
And moments when everything seems out of place;
When victory isn't so sure.
Don't be discouraged and give up the fight.
Into your darkness, He will pour out His light.
You're always safe and secure.

For nothing on earth or in heaven above
Can keep you away from His unending love.
He'll complete what He's begun.
He'll continue to mold you over the years,
So don't let the enemy stir up your fears.
With you the Lord's never done.

So offer up praise from deep down in your soul,
And remember it's knowing Him that's your goal.
Perfection's in God not in you.
And the longer you serve and walk in His ways
The less frequent will be those discouraging days;
So run 'til the race is through.

Secure in His Love

Make me a vessel fit for You to use
Let me be willing my own hopes to lose
Spill out all my selfish, sinful desire,
With Your Holy Spirit, light a new fire.

Give my heart passion to yield and to bend
Whatever my lot, whatever You send,
Let me choose joy in the midst of my pain,
For when I choose joy, Your strength is my gain.

When I am hurt, help me love and forgive,
Secure in Your love, help me to live
With rejection and hurt, unchanged by these,
Knowing it is You and not men I must please.

Teach me to take all my pain to the cross,
Grateful to share in suffering and loss,
Make my desire to give all hurts to You,
Trusting that I will be healed when I do.

Don't let me strike back in any way,
No matter what others may do or say,
Let me recall all your meek, gentle ways,
And follow Your example all of my days.

Forgetting What Lies Behind

As I press on to run this race
I cling to Your unchanging grace
Whenever I stumble, when I fall
You pick me up if I just call.

You are ever faithful, ever true.
You never change, although I do.
No one can take me from Your hand
Why that is, I can't understand

If I were You, I'd quit on me
But I'm Yours and always will be.
It seems that as long as I live
I'll be asking You to forgive

The hasty word, the careless act,
Flippant remark or lack of tact.
Though I list my sins at great length
Cover my weakness with Your strength.

The most profound truth ever taught
Heals and removes each guilty thought
And gives me hope as on I go
Jesus loves me, this I know.

For as Long as I Live

With whispers of worship or with passionate praise
I'll be calling on Jesus the rest of my days
For nothing is sweeter than moments like these
I'm lifted to heaven while still on my knees

I've cried out for mercy and He's heard my cry
And so like an eagle my spirit can fly
Above every trial, temptation, or test
Straight into His arms to find absolute rest

Where all of life's cares seem inconsequential
And only His presence and love are essential
Then cleansed and refreshed from the touch of His hand
I can rise from my knees empowered to stand

For as long as I live I must draw away
To quietly listen and reverently pray
Those moments alone with Him are life's treasure
For we were created for the Lord's pleasure

Adopted Forever

Adopted forever, abandoned, not ever
For I'm sure I'm a child of the King
Forgiven for my sin, it's grace that I walk in
And to Abba's rich promises cling

Chosen before time, His righteousness is now mine
Though I know my own unworthy heart
He still finds pleasure, and calls me His treasure
In the promise of Christ, I take part

And I will be praising that grace that's amazing
As long as I still walk on this earth
For nothing can ever his love for me sever
Or tell me that I am without worth

No personal purity earned my security
For I'm wearing His name not my own
And though I still fall short, His Spirit's in my heart
And He'll never leave me here alone

Always the Same

Our God never changes. He's always the same
He revealed that when He told us His name
He is I Am not I was or will be
That is such comfort for you and for me

Time is a dimension by which we're constrained
That was God's choice. It's what He ordained
We're but a vapor quickly passing away
But the word of the Lord always will stay

So why is this comfort to the frail human race
We who each day our mortality must face
Can we face death with no more fear than sleep?
Yes, because God has promises to keep

He who is I Am, not I was or will be
Keeps what He's promised to you and to me
And if we've accepted the gift of His grace
We can rest assured, we will see his face

In His book of life, He's written each name
Even though we fail Him, that stays the same
We are His children, not were or will be
We know His truth and so we are set free

Love Song

My soul, can you hear? It's beginning to play.
It's barely perceptible on this stormy day.
And yet, I can hear it and sway to its' beat.
In spite of my sorrow, I'm tapping my feet.

My throat choked with tears still must sing along
Whenever my heart plays the notes of His song.
For nothing on earth or in heaven above
Can stop me from singing to Him of my love.

No sorrow or burden or measure of grief
Can still the sweet symphony of my belief.
Though all my great dreams have fallen to dust
I'll still sing to Him of my hope and my trust.

Then when on the day that I draw my last breath
And pass from this life through the portals of death,
I'll hear it again playing loud, playing strong
My forever, familiar, faithful love song.

A Call to be a Man of God

Many years ago my husband, Al and I attended a weekend marriage retreat with our small group from the church we were attending. Some of the other small groups joined us there as well. We listened to some excellent teaching, and as I listened I thought about how blessed my husband and I were. Our marriage was wonderful.

Sadly, I knew that wasn't true for many of the couples sitting in the room with us. When the day's session ended, we were encouraged to write something about our spouse to share with the group the next day. I welcomed the opportunity to affirm my husband, but I know that the assignment was really hard for some of the couples. I will never forget that in one session, one of the women at the retreat described her marriage as road kill. How incredibly sad it was to hear that.

That night back in our room, I sat down to write something for Al. I know the secret to our marriage is because Christ is at the center of our relationship. Both of us have a close walk with the Lord and Christ is the glue that holds us together. Apart from the work that the Holy Spirit has done our lives, we probably would each be a mess and our own marriage might be road kill. It is amazing what God can do to change us.

The next day, I stood up to share what I had written for Al, and I prayed that the others in the room might someday if not then have the same honor and love for their mates. What I shared that day was the poem called "A Man of Integrity." I hope that if your own marriage needs healing, you and your spouse will be able to receive what you need from the Lord.

A Man of Integrity

The people that we meet are unaware
That you're a warrior whose weapon is prayer,
But I see you down on your knees.
They couldn't know how you're willing to give
The generous loving way you live.
You often give when no one sees.

If you were offered first place, you'd decline,
And stand instead at the end of the line.
You're concerned what others receive.
Nor could they know the respect you've earned,
Or all the lessons from you I've learned,
Because you live what you believe.

You are a quiet man not one who's loud.
You have a humble heart, not one that's proud.
Your character they might not see.
They might not know just how yielded you are,
But I've watched our Lord bring you so far
That it is evident to me.

It's so nice to come here and to attend
A marriage conference with my best friend.
Ours is a wonderful life.
So whether or not others ever know.
I just wanted a chance to tell you so.
I'm so grateful to be your wife.

A Love Song Well Lived

Yours is a love song that cannot be played
Instruments fail for it must be displayed
In action, not music or words
You sing it so well in all that you do
After twenty-three years, love still seems new
In my heart's where your song is heard

Writers express what they think love should be
But I've had a love song lived out for me
For so many years of my life
Your feelings for me, I don't have to doubt
For anyone who knows you soon knows about
The real love you have for your wife

I know the reason for this affection
Is that you follow God's own direction
You love because He first loved you
The secret of loving year after year
Is found by men who to God draw near
Just as you have learned how to do

Keep living your love song. I can't wait to hear
The verse you're adding for the upcoming year
May God grant us many more days
For I want to live out a love song for you
I hope that you'll hear it in all that I do
And feel it in unnumbered ways

The Test of Love

Oh, precious couple, we see you stand

Facing your tomorrows hand in hand,

So happy just to be together,

So sure there's no storm you can't weather.

Sweet, young couple, please do not assume,

You won't struggle with your bride or groom.

There will come moments when you'll be irate

Over words or actions of this mate.

Those are times to turn to God above.

He will help you pass the test of love.

When spouses behave at their own worst,

Only the cup of love can quench their thirst.

So at those moments yield your own will.

Let God allow them to drink their fill.

And if you do, I think you will learn,

That this is a favor they will return.

I know you'll be grateful when they do,

That day when the thirsty one is you.

When all that you say and do is wrong,

But they pass the test with love that's strong.

And if you are tempted not to give

Grace to the person with whom you live,

Remember that God has never ceased

To love you when you deserve it least.

Promise Keeper

He was a man like any other.
At times he could be both weak or strong
He wanted peace with every brother,
But in his life some things just went wrong.

Within his heart, in days of his youth,
Some bitter seeds of anger were sown.
And though he had sought to find God's truth,
Through passing years, those seeds had grown.

His great desire was a heart at peace.
And for that to his Father he would pray,
But from anger there was no release,
Until that one very special day.

He went to Chicago's Soldier's Field,
Where Promise Keepers met for praise,
There his troubled heart at last did yield,
To Jesus Christ who all hope does raise.

God taught him about love's test that day
And this is the lesson he truly learned
Love isn't love 'til we give it away
To the people by whom it's not earned.

He gave up his anger and all rights,

To the One who gave him His own life,

And went home with peace and shining light.

To bring joy to his family and wife.

These words are penned by that grateful wife,

Whose own love for God grows much deeper,

For He changed everything in her life,

When He gave her a promise keeper.

Tell Me the Reasons

Tell me the reasons you love me
My dear husband will often say
And so I tell him happily
It is a game we love to play

And I, too, ask for the reasons
Though I've heard them all before
In all of life's sweet seasons
Those are the moments I adore

One day the Lord spoke to my heart
Of this game of affirmation
He said He wanted me to start
To give Him appreciation

Tell Me the reasons you love Me
My spirit often hears Him say
And so I tell Him happily
It's a sweet prayer I love to pray

Under the Umbrella

What a joy it is to hear you say
That if I hurt you'll not cease to pray,
As you wrap me up in arms of love
Lifting all my cares to God above.

How could I help but find sweet release
When you faithfully kneel asking peace.
You love me as Christ loves His own bride
What comfort I find when at your side.

My darling, you are a godly man.
Our marriage works by our Lord's own plan.
You as the head over this blest wife
Provide sheltered, protected, secure life.

Twenty-two Years

For Al with love from Jan

It's been twenty-two years since I stood at your side
With the shining eyes of a young, happy bride
Deeply in love with you
The vows that were spoken and the promises made
Have been kept and commitment to love's been displayed
By the faithful things you do

We knew as we stood facing all our tomorrows
That our lives could embrace both great joy and sorrows
We've faced both hand in hand
We have both known sickness and we've been blessed by health
There have been tight money times and some days of wealth
The vows we made still stand

We've both changed very much as the years have flown by
Our love's greater than ever and we both know why
Because God has touched our lives
Twenty-two years ago I could never have guessed
That the Lord would make us so amazingly blessed
Among husbands and wives

For blessed are those on each anniversary day
Who can with grateful hearts give thanks and pray
For their husband or wife
Today I find giving that thanks easy to do
Since my greatest gift from the Lord is you
I'll love you all of my life

Man of God

Blessed is the man who has yielded his life
And how blessed are his children and his wife
That he leads them all on the narrow way
And guides each of them to seek God each day

Blessed are all of those that at work he leads
For he inspires them by his righteous deeds
How blessed are those he is willing to teach
For God's best he helps them yearn and reach

Blessed, too, are all those who call him their friend
Such a man remains faithful to the end
Blessed are the neighbors who watch and who see
A man who by the Lord has been set free

Blessed is the nation that would wisely choose
This servant of Christ as their servant to use
Yes, blessed are all by one who truly knows
He must yield his life wherever he goes

A Call to the Family

Family is very important to me. Al and I have been blessed with four children and seven precious grandchildren. I had the privilege of growing up in a home where I felt loved. My parents have both gone on now to their home in heaven, but I am still blessed to have my sister, Elaine, and my brother, Bob. Many of my sweetest childhood memories are of the time I spent with our maternal grandmother. We simply called her Gram. I'm sure Bob and Elaine have wonderful memories of her, too. She was a humble, loving woman of faith. I spent so many hours with her baking cookies and talking. She taught me so much about love, kindness, perseverance, and faith in the midst of trials. She was a living example to me of a servant of Christ.

I was 12 years old when my grandmother told me the story of the room full of crosses that I talk about in the poem I called "The Gift." I was going through a hard time at school and suffering a lot of teasing by classmates. Gram told me the story, and it helped me to put things in perspective. I think she had read the story somewhere, but I have no idea where. Throughout my life that story has been a gift to me whenever I am walking through trials of any kind. One Christmas my husband bought me a little jeweled cross and when I wear it, I think of Gram and the room full of crosses.

I am a blessed woman to have known Louise Taylor as Gram. It is my heartfelt prayer that someday my own grandchildren will feel that they had a grandmother who was a woman of faith and who loved them dearly just as I had in Gram.

The Gift

Once as a girl in emotional pain
I turned to my grandmother to complain
About my difficult days
She listened to my tearful tale of woe
I knew she would for she loved me so
And I wondered what she'd say

I was seeking a sympathetic ear
And for the understanding words I'd hear
She gave me a gift that day
A story of a young woman in pain
Who approached the throne of God to complain
About grief on the narrow way

She moaned her cross was too heavy to bear
And begged Him to lift it in her prayer
So He led her through a door
To a room filled with all kinds of crosses
That represent our sorrows and losses
To pick one was now her chore

Choose, my daughter, the burden you will bear
About your pain, you know I truly care
So I'll let you make the choice
She looked at the crosses of every kind
Being careful before she made up her mind
One would make her heart rejoice

Some great crosses she couldn't lift at all
And some when she lifted them, made her fall
Others made her writhe in pain
But finally upon a shelf of gold
Was a jeweled cross of beauty untold
On a fragile golden chain

She opened the clasp and put it on
And all of her pain seemed suddenly gone
Her heart was bursting with song
Father, this one is just right for me
I know that, my daughter, for you see
You've carried it all along

So, as I have journeyed throughout this life
In those times of trial and days of strife
I've remembered what I was told
Though my sorrows and grief seem hard to bear
I thank God my grandmother made me aware
They're my tiny cross of gold

The Carpenter's Hands

The carpenter's hands accustomed to wood
Hardened and calloused by work that is good
Now moved softly as a dove
Hands taught to move with hammer and saw
Now moved with gentleness and with awe
Made gentle by great love

For those hardened hands now held his son
One precious new life that had just begun
The miracle of birth
The look in his eyes said "I'll be there for you
To keep you safe in all you do.
How much your life is worth."

No more important job is ever done
Than being a good father to a son,
Helping him find his way.
And each action taken, each spoken word
Will be carefully watched and carefully heard
By his new son each day.

Yes, into his calloused carpenter's hands
Has been placed great trust and he understands
The task before him now.
But held in another Carpenter's hands
He will be able to meet all these demands
For He will show him how.

Storm Song

Lord, we're facing rough water

This son and this daughter

As winds drive us on through a storm.

With the swell of each wave

We don't feel very brave

But we know You can keep us from harm.

And we're fighting our fears

And we're drying our tears

As our trembling lips offer You praise.

For we've studied and heard

And hidden Your Word

In our hearts for these difficult days.

With prayers of thanksgiving

We both can keep living

For You are the Beacon of Light.

And we can keep sailing

Though our strength is failing

For we're safely upheld by Your might.

May we give You glory

As we tell the story

Of how we found You there in the night.

The waves rose around us

But Your strong arms found us

And darkness gave way to the Light.

Legacy of Love

A protestant girl knelt at a Catholic shrine
"God my heart breaks for this baby's not really mine."
She couldn't face giving him to parents unknown
This foster child that she'd learned to love as her own

She prayed to this God that she really didn't know
And He heard from heaven and let His love flow
Peace filled up her heart and then she knew she could face
Separation from the child; God gave her His grace

So she prepared an album of pictures for those
That she didn't know, but who were the parents God chose
And she prayed for them, too, and for her little boy
She had no idea of God's plan for her joy

God granted a miracle to her great surprise
She heard the good news and tears welled up in her eyes
It was decided that she could adopt this son
She could barely believe, God let her be the one

But the greatest gift was not this infant son
The greatest gift was what she knew God had done
He had shown her Himself, His love and His care
For most of her life, she had been unaware

It took desperation to make her call His name
But from that day forth, she was never the same
Of her new life in Christ, this prayer had been the start
For God soon showed her how He could live in her heart

Twenty-eight years have gone by; the boy is a man
And now she can see much of God's wonderful plan
For the faith that she found on that day long ago
Has been passed on to her son and she watches it grow

Her son's children, too, now hear of God's gracious love
And are taught that He hears every prayer sent above
A heritage of faith to pass to future generations
A legacy of love from the God of creation

A Mother's Love

I know your pain for it's one I have known
The longing to hold a child of your own,
To have a little one call you Mother,
A precious sound that is like no other.

Your arms ache to hold. Your lips yearn to kiss
These are the dreams that to you are bliss.
You want to share all that you know,
And help a little one to learn and grow.

My daughter, you've faced a difficult test
And passed it by saying, "God knows best",
And telling me, "Mom, His plan I see.
He has some children who are just for me."

You will open your heart to do child care,
And meet the needs of which you're aware.
You'll pray for the grace to let each of them go
And when the time comes, how your tears may flow.

But for the joy of love you'll risk the pain,
And in spite of loss there will be gain
Though you care first for one child then another
God will have truly made you a mother.

Lifelong Friend

I have known my best friend since the day of my birth.

We've been sisters and friends all my days on this earth.

When I was born, she was only seven years old.

But she loved me from the start. I know. I've been told.

We've laughed and we've cried, and we've talked for hours on end.

We've argued and fought, but we've always stayed friends.

This friendship's a blessing from our Father above,

Because of this priceless gift, I've always had love.

Life's heartaches and sorrows and real pain I've known,

But no matter what came I've not faced it alone.

For me there has always been a hand I could hold

And the warmth of a hug that could ward off the cold.

This relationship's worth is far beyond measure.

It is one thing I'm sure that I always will treasure.

Of all the blessings God could have chosen to send,

I'm so grateful He gave me a true lifelong friend.

A Call to Christ at Christmas

No room! What sad words those are. No room in the inn for the Savior of the world. Every Christmas season, it makes Christians feel so sorrowful that all that was offered to Christ at His birth was a manger in a stable. We often think that if only that innkeeper knew who it was that He was sending to his stable that he would have found some room inside. And not only some room, but surely he would have offered the best room in the inn or perhaps his own quarters.

One Christmas as I was thinking about that innkeeper, I realized that you can know who Jesus is and still not make room for him. We do it all the time. We get caught up in all the rushing around keeping ourselves busy and fail to make room for the Savior in our own lives. We push our quiet times of prayer, meditation, and Bible study to the back burner. However, many of the things we still manage to squeeze into our schedules are not really so important. We find time to be online, time to watch TV, time for sports, time for our friends and family, time to read, time to work on our homes, and time for countless other pursuits. There is nothing wrong with spending time on any of those things, but shouldn't time with Jesus be at the top of the list? I think that as believers we know it should, but it is so easy to get sidetracked. We need to make a conscious commitment to prioritize making room in our lives for our Lord.

I wanted to remember this and so I wrote the poem called "No Room." Maybe it will help you to remember, too. Clear your calendar and spend some time with the Lord. You will be glad you did.

No Room

No recognition of Your great worth
Was offered at Your Bethlehem birth.
There was no room and men were not able
To offer more than a simple stable.

At Christmas our eyes mist with tears,
As we look back over two thousand years.
We often arrogantly assume
We'd no longer tell You there's no room.

But that is exactly what we say,
As busy men and women today.
No room for a quiet time with You.
We think we have too much to do.

There's no room within the hectic lives
Of all these harried husbands and wives,
Who teach their children life on the run
In twenty-four hours You don't get one.

Why do we willingly keep this pace
That is exhausting the human race?
We must repent of this behavior
And make room for You, our dear Savior.

If we take time for prayerful reflection,
You'll give us purpose and direction,
Intimate moments alone with You,
Will brighten everything else we do.

Holding Heaven's Gift

So long ago, so far away in Bethlehem of old
Mary wrapped the Gift of Heaven to keep Him from the cold
And gently lay her newborn son to sleep upon the hay
The Son of God so humbly slept on that first Christmas Day

How quietly the gift of peace came to men on earth
The treasure of the universe, the pearl of greatest worth
To us the greatest gift was given that ever we'll receive
It's ours to hold and ours to keep, if we will just believe

A humble manger no longer holds the blessed virgin's son
And many are the lives He's changed, indeed my own is one
For He has chosen His own place and I am set apart
Forever He is resting in the hollow of my heart

But what is more, He's held within each and every one
Who reaches out to receive the gift of God's own Son
As humble hearts are holding Him, yes, just as He has planned
He's really holding us in the hollow of His hand

Merry Christmas

Sometimes I'm still startled by the sound
Of lighthearted laughter all around.
I hear the sound and then I rejoice,
Because it's your laughter. It's your voice.

I'm amazed as I watch when you touch
A friend with words that are needed much.
And I strain to listen. I want to hear
Your words of wisdom that are so dear.

And when I'm there to hear your prayers,
It lifts my burdens; lessens my cares.
The changes that God has wrought in you
Give me hope for I need changes, too.

We should be merry and I'm able
Thanks to the gift from Bethlehem's stable.
Emmanuel, God with us, His name
And since He's with you, you're not the same.

Yes, you are truly one special reason
To celebrate this Christmas season,
He's come to you and changed your life,
You're a Christmas present to your wife.

Merry Christmas, Al
All my love,
Jan

The Camels are Coming

Mary and Joseph could never have guessed
The plan that God had for His Child to be blessed
Until the day camels arrived from afar
Because wise men followed a bright shining star

God met His Son's needs, so we have been told
With frankincense, myrrh, and glittering gold
And He's still meeting needs of those that He loves
With plans only known in heaven above

So if there are times in the upcoming year
When difficult days cause your heart to fear
Just look at this camel and think of the day
God provided in a miraculous way

And know that He'll always provide for you, too
Even when you can't imagine what He can do
Like Mary and Joseph, you'll never have guessed
The way that He'll work things for you to be blessed

Wise Men

In David's City so long ago
Beneath a shining star's brilliant glow
Wise men knelt before a newborn King
Gifts and reverent worship to bring

In our own city not long ago
In the early morning light's soft glow
A wise man knelt before that same King
Sweet, praise and reverent worship to bring

Arising at the first light of day
I came upon you kneeling to pray
And knew I was seeing the real reason
That we celebrate the Christmas season

And I know that I am a blessed wife
Whose own husband leads this kind of life
And wisely starts to live a new day
By first bowing down to humbly pray

This year as we recall Christ's birth
I'll think about how He's still on earth
Within hearts of men who realize
That dependence on God makes them wise